SUMMER SKILLS 2

DAILY ACTIVITY WORKBOOK

For the Child Going into SECOND GRADE

Written by **SHANNON KEELEY**

Illustrations by **PATRICIA STORMS**

Cover illustration by Amy Vangsgard

Flash Kids
A Division of Barnes & Noble
122 Fifth Avenue
New York, NY 10011

ISBN: 978-1-4114-9829-7

Please submit all inquiries to FlashKids@bn.com

Printed and bound in China

5 7 9 11 13 15 14 12 10 8 6 4

DEAR PARENT,

As a parent, you want your child to have time to relax and have fun during the summer, but you don't want your child's math and reading skills to get rusty. How do you make time for summer fun and also ensure that your child will be ready for the next school year?

This *Summer Skills Daily Activity Workbook* provides short, fun activities in reading and math to help children keep their skills fresh all summer long. This book not only reviews what children learned during first grade, it also introduces what they'll be learning in second grade. The numbered daily activities make it easy for children to complete one activity a day and stay on track the whole summer long. Best of all, the games, puzzles, and stories help children retain their knowledge as well as build new skills. By the time your child finishes the book, he or she will be ready for a smooth transition into second grade.

As your child completes the activities in this book, shower him or her with encouragement and praise. You can feel good knowing that you are taking an active and important role in your child's education. Helping your child complete the activities in this book is providing him or her with an excellent example—that you value learning, every day! Have a wonderful summer, and most of all, have fun learning together!

Visit us at *www.flashkidsbooks.com* for free downloads, informative articles, and valuable parent resources!

ALPHABOATS

Write the letters that come before and after.

1. e f g

2. ___ r ___

3. ___ j ___

4. ___ v ___

5. ___ d ___

6. ___ h ___

7. ___ n ___

8. ___ t ___

9. ___ l ___

10. ___ p ___

11. ___ y ___

12. ___ b ___

In each row, cross out the letter that is not in ABC order.

13. A B C ~~X~~ D E F G

14. L M N O B P Q R

15. T U V W X Y S Z

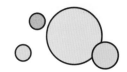

JOKE TIME

Write the numbers that come before and after.

_3_ 4 _5_   ___ 9 ___   ___ 19 ___
A   L   B   T   E   O

___ 12 ___   ___ 7 ___   ___ 15 ___
T   P   Y   I   W   C

Unscramble each set of numbers and write them in order from smallest to biggest.

16 13 14 12 15   _12_ ___ ___ ___ ___
                   H   K   R   E   S

22 25 21 23 24   ___ ___ ___ ___ ___
                   D   C   O   G   U

Now unscramble and write the numbers from biggest to smallest.

7 4 5 8 6   _8_ ___ ___ ___ ___
             J   N   S   A   T

18 16 20 17 19   ___ ___ ___ ___ ___
                  M   E   V   R   X

Find each number above and write the letter to complete the joke.

Where do numbers like to eat lunch?

_A_ ___   ___ ___ ___
3   10   11   12   15

___ ___ ___ ___ ___ ___ ___
22   23   25   7   4   19   17

THE FIRST FERRIS WHEEL

Read the story. Then answer the questions.

George W. Ferris was a man with big ideas. In 1893, a big fair was being planned in Chicago. George built a ride that looked like a giant wheel. It was 250 feet wide and held 60 people. They called it the Ferris wheel.

1. What is this passage about?
   a) the first Ferris wheel
   b) the first fair

2. How wide was the Ferris wheel?
   a) 250 feet
   b) 60 feet

3. Who was George W. Ferris?
   a) The first man to go to the fair
   b) The man who built the first Ferris wheel

4. Why was the ride called a "Ferris wheel"?
   a) Because 60 people could ride it
   b) Because George Ferris built it

PRETTY PATTERNS

Repeat the patterns.

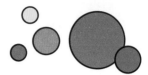

WORD SEARCH

Find the words and circle them. Words can go across or down.

again	know	live	any	when
put	after	every	could	then

o a g a i n o o

o f a n l y c u

e t n y t p u t

v e k w h a t h

e r n l i v e e

r c o u l d v n

y o w h e n r y

Day 5:
Sight Words

 # ADD AND CIRCLE

Add. Circle the number that is bigger in each box.

1. 4   5
    + 3 + 1

2. 2   4
    + 6 + 0

3. 1   3
    + 7 + 3

4. 0   2
    + 5 + 2

5. 4   2
    + 1 + 8

6. 1   8
    + 6 + 1

7. 5   5
    + 4 + 5

8. 0   3
    + 9 + 7

A FRIEND TO THE END

A **telling** sentence ends with a period:

> I have no lunch.

An **asking** sentence ends with a question mark.

> Do you want some?

End each sentence with a period or a question mark.

1. Where is your lunch _?_

2. I left my lunch at home ___

3. I can share my lunch ___

4. Do you like apples ___

5. Can I have a bite ___

6. You are a good friend ___

MAZE CAFÉ

Count by 5s to find your way through the maze. Follow the trail and see what's for lunch at the café!

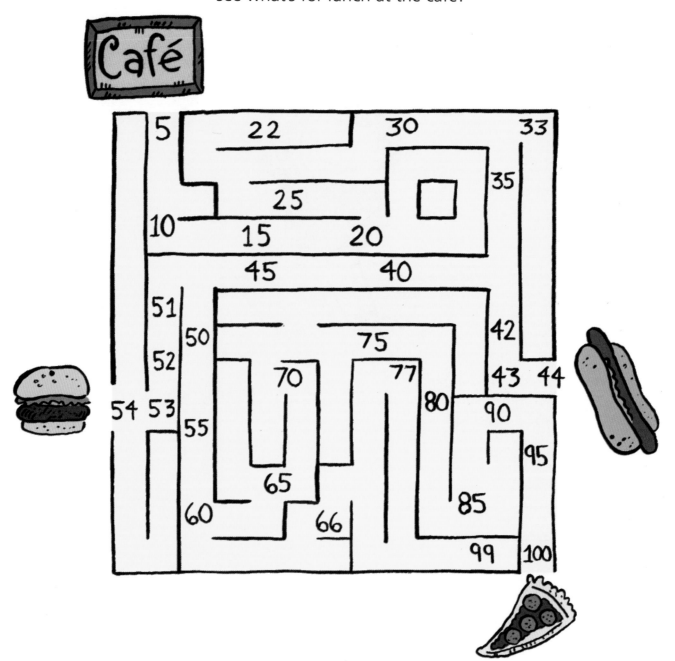

Count by 5s.

5	10			25			40		
		65			80				100

SHOW AND TELL

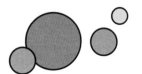
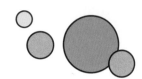

Complete the telling sentences about the picture. Then write one of your own.

1. This is my pet bird ☐

2. The bird _____

_____

3. _____

What would you ask the boy about his bird? Complete the asking sentences.
Then write one of your own.

4. What does the bird eat ☐

5. How _____

6. _____

_____

Day 9:
Telling and Asking

SPACE RACE

Subtract. Find the answer on the space race and cross it out.
See which rocket gets to the moon first!

1.	8 − 4 4	**2.**	5 − 2

3.	4 − 2	**4.**	9 − 3

9   10
1   7
5   8
3   6
4   2

5.	9 − 1	**6.**	10 − 5

7.	6 − 5	**8.**	9 − 2

A   B

9.	9 − 0	**10.**	12 − 2

LOTS OF LETTERS

Write the beginning and the ending letters.

1.

_s_ i _x_

2.

___ u ___

3.

___ a ___

4.

___ a ___

5.

___ e ___

6.

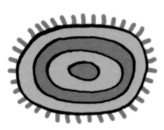

___ i ___

7.

___ i ___

8.

___ u ___

9.

___ a ___

If the two pictures have the same beginning sound, circle **beginning**.
If they have the same ending sound, circle **ending**.

10.

Beginning

Ending

11.

Beginning

Ending

12.

Beginning

Ending

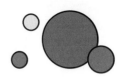

CLOWNING AROUND

Write the missing numbers from 51 to 100.

51	52	T __	54	R __	56	57	T __	A __	60
U __	62	63	64	B __	66	L __	68	69	N __
71	O __	S __	74	75	E __	77	78	N __	80
D __	82	83	F __	85	86	P __	88	89	D __
91	O __	93	94	V __	E __	97	E __	99	100

Find each number above and
write the letter to complete the joke.

How high did the silly clown count?

T __ __ __ __ __
53 92   72 70 98

__ __ __ __ __ __ __
84 61 79 81 55 96 90

MINI GOLF

Number the sentences to show the order of events in the story.

_____ The course started with some easy holes.

_____ Andy and his friends went to the mini golf course.

_____ The hole was on a narrow bridge above the water.

_____ They rented clubs and balls and started the game.

_____ Andy's ball rolled off the bridge and splashed into the water.

_____ Then they got to a very tricky hole surrounded by water.

Connect each word with its meaning.

1. course   **a)** to pay money to use something

2. rented   **b)** not very wide

3. tricky   **c)** a series of challenges

4. narrow   **d)** difficult

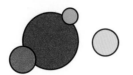 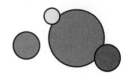

COIN COUNT

Circle the coin or the coins that equal the value on the left.

1¢			
5¢			
10¢			
25¢			
10¢			
15¢			

HAPPY ENDINGS

Complete each sentence with the singular or the plural word.
Use the picture clues and the word box to help.

ribbon	tree	sock	wheel
fox	bike	tire	rock

1. I found my lucky racing _____.

2. It was time for the _____ race!

3. I raced along a path lined with _____.

4. I saw two _____ playing in the woods.

5. There were sharp _____ on the ground.

6. I thought that I had a flat _____.

7. It was just a rock stuck in my _____.

8. I finished the race and got a _____.

FLIP OUT!

Add. Then flip the numbers in each equation and add again.

You can swap the numbers you're adding and get the same answer!

$$3 + 4 = 7 \longrightarrow 4 + 3 = 7$$

1. $2 + 3 = \underline{5}$

   $\underline{3} + \underline{2} = \underline{5}$

2. $6 + 4 = \underline{\hphantom{00}}$

   $\underline{\hphantom{00}} + \underline{\hphantom{00}} = \underline{\hphantom{00}}$

3. $5 + 2 = \underline{\hphantom{00}}$

   $\underline{\hphantom{00}} + \underline{\hphantom{00}} = \underline{\hphantom{00}}$

4. $2 + 9 = \underline{\hphantom{00}}$

   $\underline{\hphantom{00}} + \underline{\hphantom{00}} = \underline{\hphantom{00}}$

5. $6 + 3 = \underline{\hphantom{00}}$

   $\underline{\hphantom{00}} + \underline{\hphantom{00}} = \underline{\hphantom{00}}$

6. $9 + 1 = \underline{\hphantom{00}}$

   $\underline{\hphantom{00}} + \underline{\hphantom{00}} = \underline{\hphantom{00}}$

7. $7 + 5 = \underline{\hphantom{00}}$

   $\underline{\hphantom{00}} + \underline{\hphantom{00}} = \underline{\hphantom{00}}$

8. $3 + 8 = \underline{\hphantom{00}}$

   $\underline{\hphantom{00}} + \underline{\hphantom{00}} = \underline{\hphantom{00}}$

SUNNY SENTENCES

Use capitals for:

- First word of a sentence
- The word "I"
- Places
- People's names

This summer **I** went to **H**awaii with **A**my.

Rewrite each sentence with correct capitalization.

1. we got on the plane in los angeles.

We got on the plane in Los Angeles.

2. our plane landed in honolulu.

_____

3. then amy and i flew to maui.

_____

4. amy's sister peg lives in maui.

_____

5. peg took amy and me swimming.

_____

6. i want to go to hawaii again!

_____

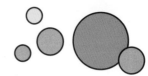

SPEEDY SUMS

Circle the equations that equal the number in the car at the top.
Then write some of your own equations that equal the same sum.

8	**12**	**6**	**11**
(5 + 3)	4 + 8	2 + 4	7 + 4
12 − 4	11 − 1	12 − 6	11 − 0
4 + 4	10 + 2	6 + 6	9 + 3
10 − 3	14 − 2	14 − 7	12 − 1
7 + 2	7 + 6	0 + 6	5 + 6
16 − 8	15 − 3	10 − 4	10 − 1
___ + ___	___ + ___	___ + ___	___ + ___
___ − ___	___ − ___	___ − ___	___ − ___
___ − ___	___ − ___	___ − ___	___ − ___

POOL PARTY

List things you see in and around the pool:

_____ _____ _____ _____

_____ _____ _____ _____

_____ _____ _____ _____

Describe the kids. What are they doing and wearing?

_____

_____

_____

_____

What kind of day is it?

_____

_____

TEAM TIMES

Write the time below each clock. Find the time on the racetrack and cross it out. See which team goes all the way!

COBRAS 10:~~00~~ - 2:30 - 4:30 - 11:00 - 12:30

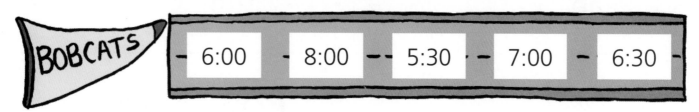

BOBCATS 6:00 - 8:00 - 5:30 - 7:00 - 6:30

1.

10:00

2.

_____

3.

_____

4.

_____

5.

_____

6.

_____

7.

_____

8.

_____

9.

_____

THE LONG AND SHORT OF IT

Add **e** to make the long vowel sound.

1.

cap   c a p e

2.

tub   _ _ _ _

3.

can   _ _ _ _

4.

tap   _ _ _ _

Add or take away the **e** to change the vowel sound.

5. h i d   hide

6. hop   _ _ _ _

7. fin   _ _ _ _

8. _ _ _ _   bite

9. _ _ _ _   note

10. mop   _ _ _ _

11. _ _ _ _   made

12. rod   _ _ _ _

 # ADD-VENTURE TIME!

Add the three numbers and write the answer.

1. 2 4 + 1 **B**	**2.** 5 2 + 2 **E**	**3.** 2 3 + 3 **N**
4. 4 2 + 4 **I**	**5.** 8 3 + 3 **L**	**6.** 6 3 + 2 **C**
7. 9 3 + 1 **E**	**8.** 3 4 + 5 **!**	**9.** 7 5 + 3 **T**

Find each number in the answers above and write the matching letter to complete the joke.

What did the 0 say to the 8?

N ___ ___ ___
8   10   11   9

___ ___ ___ ___ ___
7   13   14   15   12

LARRY AND GARY

Read the story. Then answer the questions.

Larry and Gary wanted to do something special for their mother's birthday. Their mother loved flowers. Larry was artistic, so he painted a picture of a flower garden. Gary had good business ideas, so he started a lemonade stand. With the money he earned, he bought

his mother some flowers. Both boys had worked hard to give their mother nice gifts. She had a very happy birthday!

Check whether the statement describes Larry, Gary, or both boys.

	Larry	Gary	Both
1. Wanted to do something special			X
2. Was very artistic			
3. Earned money to buy flowers			
4. Worked hard to give a nice present			
5. Painted a picture of a flower garden			
6. Had good business ideas			

**Day 23:
Comparing Characters**

DO YOU MEASURE UP?

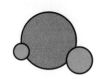

Use the ruler to measure each line, and write it below.

Use the ruler to draw lines that equal the numbers below.

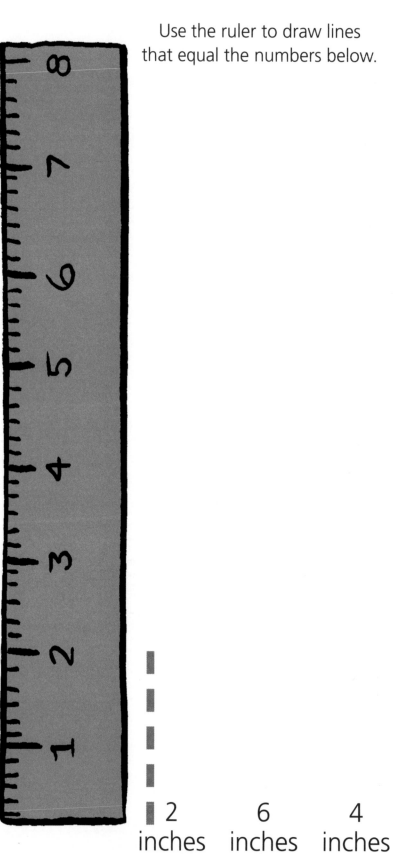

3 inches

_____ inches

_____ inches

2 inches

6 inches

4 inches

WACKY WORDS

Draw a line to connect the word parts.

rain	room
bed	fly
snow	ball
butter	bow
side	man
foot	walk

Write the word that goes with the picture clues. Use the words from above.

1. [butter image] + [fly image]

_____

2. [foot image] + [ball image]

_____

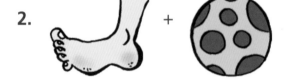

3. 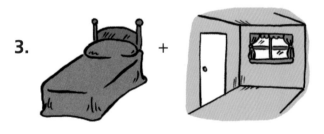 [bed image] + [room image]

_____

4.  [snow image] + [man image]

_____

5.  → [square image] + [girl walking image]

_____

6. [rain image] + [bow image]

_____

MATH MUNCHIES

Add or subtract to solve the problems.

1. Andy has 3 apples, and Sue has 2. How many apples do they have altogether?

_____ apples

2. Steve had 8 cookies. He gave 4 to Brian. How many cookies does Steve have now?

_____ cookies

3. Alex has 5 mushrooms and 6 peppers on his pizza slice. How many toppings does he have altogether?

_____ toppings

4. Sara had 15 french fries, and she gave 5 to Jason. How many fries does Sara have left?

_____ fries

5. Jane has 6 blueberries. Her dad gave her 6 strawberries. How many berries does she have altogether?

_____ berries

6. Bob had 12 chips in the bag. He dropped 4 on the ground. How many chips are left?

_____ chips

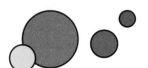
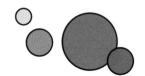

NAME THAT NOUN

A **noun** is a person, a place, or a thing.

Tom reads **books** at **school**.

Circle the words that are nouns.

write   boy   cap   sit

smart   pencil   paper   read

Now write some nouns you see in the picture:

_____   _____   _____

Circle the noun in each sentence.

1. Sit quietly at your desk.

2. Open your book, please.

3. Take out a pen.

4. Use some paper for writing.

HELPING HANDS

Draw the hands on each clock to show the time.

1. 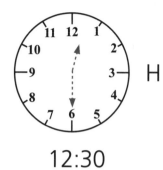 H

12:30

2. 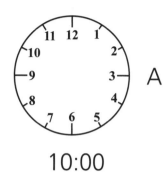 A

10:00

3. 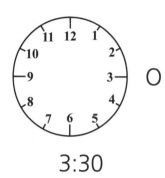 O

3:30

4. 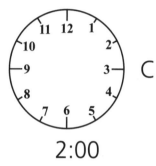 C

2:00

5. 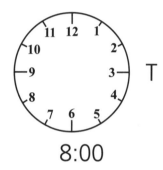 T

8:00

6. 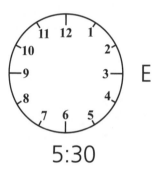 E

5:30

7. 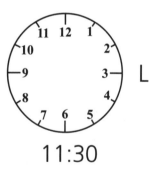 L

11:30

8. 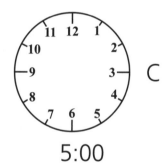 C

5:00

9. 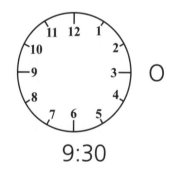 O

9:30

Look at the arrows, and find the clock above that matches.
Write the letter on the line to read the message.

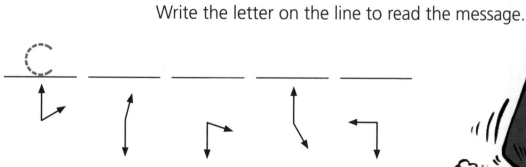

STORY TIME

Write the beginning, the middle, and the ending of the story to go along with the pictures.

Beginning

_____

_____

_____

_____

_____

Middle

_____

_____

_____

_____

_____

Ending

_____

_____

_____

_____

_____

Now write a title for your story.

_____

RACE TRACKS

Add the numbers to solve each problem.
Circle the track whose equations all have the same answer.

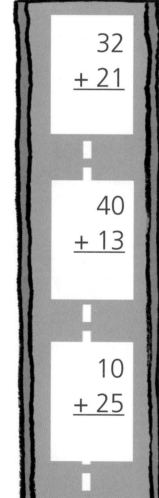

$$32 + 21$$

$$40 + 13$$

$$10 + 25$$

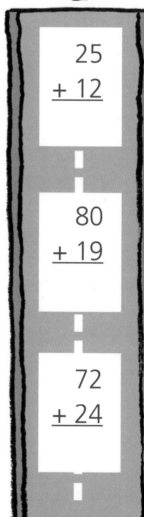

$$25 + 12$$

$$80 + 19$$

$$72 + 24$$

$$42 + 36$$

$$14 + 64$$

$$53 + 25$$

A LONG WAY TO GO

Write the vowels to complete each word.

a_e	ai	ay	ee
ea	oa	ow	oe
o_e	ie	y	
I_e	ue	u_e	

1.

r o s e

2.

b___ ___

3.

r___ ___n

4.
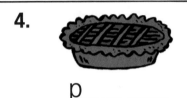
p___ ___

5.

b___k___

6.
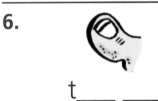
t___ ___

7.
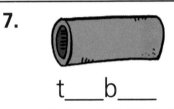
t___b___

8.

cr___

9.

gl___ ___

10.
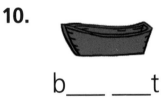
b___ ___t

11.

h___ ___

12.

b___ ___

13.

c___k___

14.
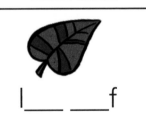
l___ ___f

List the words from above under the correct vowel sound.

long a	long e	long i	long o	long u
_____	_____	_____	_____	_____
_____	_____	_____	_____	_____
_____		_____	_____	
			_____	

NUMBER FUN

Count by 2s. Write the missing numbers.

	F		N	
2	____	6	____	10
O		R	E	
____	14	____	____	20
T	H		E	
____	____	26	____	30

Count by 10s. Write the missing numbers.

		I	S	
10	20	____	____	50
U	T			
____	____	80	90	100

Find each number above and write the letter to complete the joke.

Where did the numbers have a picnic?

I ___ ___ ___ ___
30 8   70 24 18

___ ___ ___ ___ ___ ___ ___
4   12 60 16 28 40 70

BONNIE'S BOAT TRIP

Read the story. Then answer the questions.

Bonnie's boat slowly crept through the murky water. She paddled toward a shady tree to get out of the blazing sun. A snake dozed high in the tree's branches. Mosquitoes buzzed above the steamy water. Bonnie waited quietly in the thick, damp air. Suddenly, a scaly green tail flashed through the water. Bonnie got her camera ready. She had been waiting all day to get a picture of an alligator.

1. What is the setting?
   a) a forest
   b) a swamp
   c) a desert

2. What kinds of animals live here?

_____

_____

3. What is the weather like?

_____

_____

4. Draw a picture to show the setting of the story.

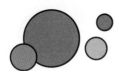

TAKING SIDES

Count the number of sides and corners on each shape.
Circle the shape that does not belong.

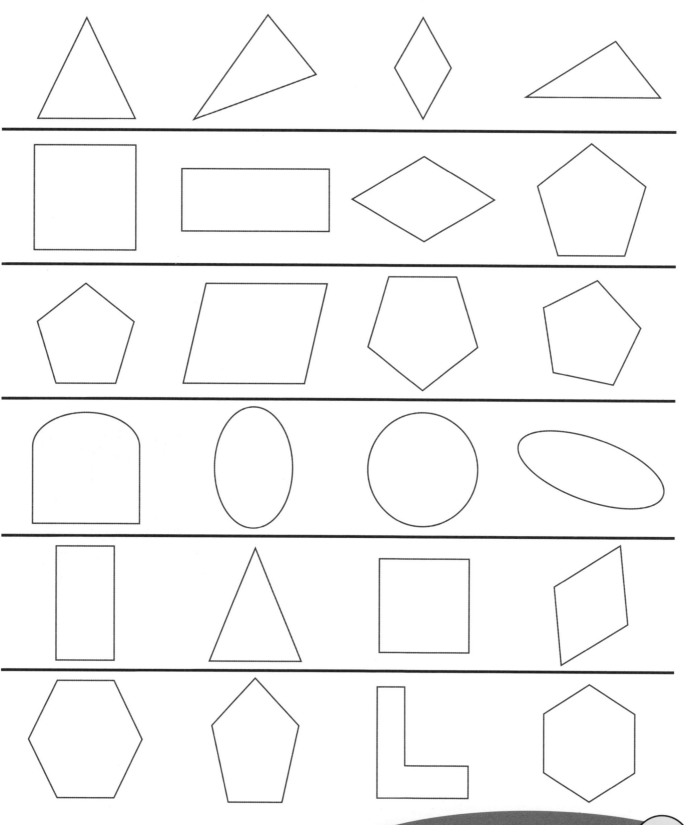

PUTTING IT TOGETHER

Draw a line to connect each contraction with the two words it comes from.

can't	are not
won't	could not
isn't	will not
aren't	is not
couldn't	did not
didn't	can not

Underline the two words that can make a contraction.
Write the contraction on the line.

1. I <u>did not</u> wake up today. _didn't_

2. I could not hear the alarm. _____

3. I can not be late to school. _____

4. My parents are not going to like this. _____

5. The bus is not going to wait. _____

6. I will not get to school on time! _____

FIGURE IT OUT

Compare the numbers and the equations and write **<**, **>**, or **=**.
Use each sign one time for each box.

1.   3 ☐ 30

21 ☐ 21

44 ☐ 14

2.   10 ☐ 3 + 1

6 ☐ 5 + 4

8 ☐ 3 + 5

3.   2 + 1 ☐ 2 + 2

3 + 4 ☐ 6 + 0

2 + 8 ☐ 8 + 2

4.   7 + 1 ☐ 4 + 5

5 + 1 ☐ 3 + 3

4 + 2 ☐ 3 + 1

5.   5 − 3 ☐ 6 − 2

8 − 3 ☐ 7 − 5

6 − 3 ☐ 10 − 7

6.   8 − 7 ☐ 5 − 4

4 − 0 ☐ 7 − 4

8 − 8 ☐ 7 − 2

7.   1 + 4 ☐ 10 − 5

6 + 2 ☐ 6 − 3

2 + 0 ☐ 10 − 7

8.   10 − 4 ☐ 4 + 4

9 − 5 ☐ 2 + 2

6 − 1 ☐ 3 + 0

ACTION-PACKED PARTY

A **verb** is an action word.

She **blows** out the candles.

Circle the words that are verbs.

cake   sing   birthday   clap

party   candles   melt   blow

Now write some action words you see in the picture:

_____   _____   _____

Circle the verb in each sentence.

1. Molly closes her eyes.

2. Her friends shout, "Happy Birthday!"

3. Everyone eats a lot of cake.

4. Then Molly opens her gifts.

**Day 37:
Verbs**

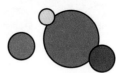

SPELL IT OUT

Solve each equation. Write the answer as a word in the puzzle.

Across

2. 5 + 1 = _____

3. 8 − 7 = _____

4. 10 − 2 = _____

6. 3 + 7 = _____

8. 11 − 6 = _____

Down

1. 9 − 7 = _____

2. 2 + 5 = _____

5. 9 − 6 = _____

7. 3 + 6 = _____

8. 12 − 8 = _____

READ AND WRITE!

Choose a storybook from home or the library.
Read the book and answer the questions below.

Book title: _____

Author: _____

The story takes place in _____.

The characters in the book are _____

_____.

This is what happens in the story. First _____

_____.

Then, _____

_____.

Finally, _____

_____.

My favorite part was when _____

_____.

Now draw a picture of your favorite part.

Day 39:
Writing a Book Report

RABBIT RACE

Subtract the numbers. Cross off each answer in the racetrack as you go.
See which bunny makes it all the way to the carrots!

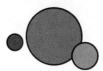

| ~~13~~ | 32 | 42 | 81 | 16 |

| 22 | 52 | 11 | 70 | 61 |

1.
$$\begin{array}{r} 17 \\ -\ 4 \\ \hline 13 \end{array}$$

2.
$$\begin{array}{r} 24 \\ -\ 2 \\ \hline \end{array}$$

3.
$$\begin{array}{r} 58 \\ -\ 6 \\ \hline \end{array}$$

4.
$$\begin{array}{r} 35 \\ -\ 3 \\ \hline \end{array}$$

5.
$$\begin{array}{r} 47 \\ -\ 5 \\ \hline \end{array}$$

6.
$$\begin{array}{r} 88 \\ -\ 7 \\ \hline \end{array}$$

7.
$$\begin{array}{r} 19 \\ -\ 8 \\ \hline \end{array}$$

8.
$$\begin{array}{r} 73 \\ -\ 3 \\ \hline \end{array}$$

9.
$$\begin{array}{r} 66 \\ -\ 5 \\ \hline \end{array}$$

RHYME AND RIDDLE

Write two words that rhyme with the first word.
Then write the short or the long vowel below the words.

1. hat

bat
cat

short a

2. pen

_____
_____

3. sit

_____
_____

4. mop

_____
_____

5. mug

_____
_____

6. bake

_____
_____

7. heat

_____
_____

8. dine

_____
_____

9. rope

_____
_____

10. true

_____
_____

Solve each riddle with a rhyming word.

11. When you hike, be sure to pack
some water and a tasty _____.

12. The sun goes down. The time is soon
when you can see the stars and _____.

13. It's time for you to go to bed.
Lie down and rest your sleepy _____.

14. It's now time to clean up the room.
You'll need a dust pan and a _____.

FUNNY MONEY

Connect the coin groups with equal value.

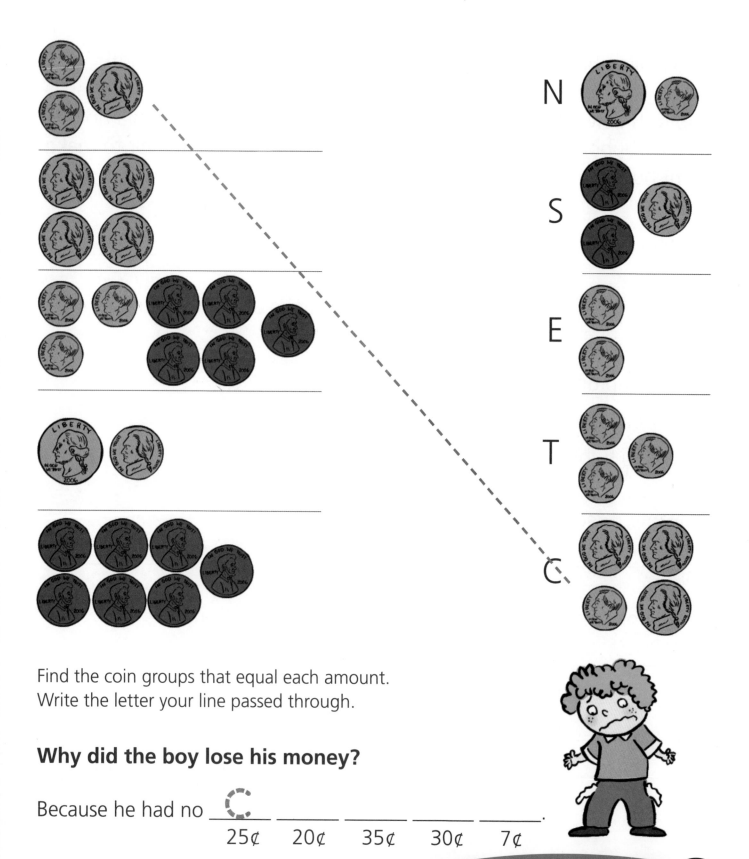

Find the coin groups that equal each amount.
Write the letter your line passed through.

Why did the boy lose his money?

Because he had no C ____ ____ ____ ____ .
                   25¢   20¢   35¢   30¢   7¢

BUBBLE FUN

Read the story. Then answer the questions.

Bubbles are the most popular toy in the world. In fact, people buy 200 million bottles a year! You can make your own bubble solution at home. Pour one gallon of water into a large tub or tray. Then mix in $\frac{2}{3}$ cup dish detergent. You can use a can, a hanger, or even a hula hoop as your bubble wand. Dip it into the tray and wave it in the air to make giant bubbles.

1. How many bottles of bubbles are sold each year? _____

2. Circle the two ingredients you need to make a bubble solution.

   a) 1 gallon dish detergent

   b) $\frac{2}{3}$ cup dish detergent

   c) 1 gallon water

   d) 200 bubbles

3. Name three things you can use for a bubble wand.

_____   _____   _____

4. Number the steps for making bubble solution at home.

_____ Mix in $\frac{2}{3}$ cup of dish detergent.

_____ Pour a gallon of water into a large tray.

_____ Wave it in the air.

_____ Dip a can, a hanger, or a hula hoop into the mixture.

SWAP AND SUBTRACT

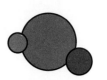

You can swap the numbers in an equation and get the same answer!

$$2 + 1 = 3 \rightarrow 1 + 2 = 3$$
$$3 - 1 = 2 \rightarrow 3 - 2 = 1$$

Fill in the missing numbers to solve the equations.

1. $4 + 2 = $ _____

$2 + $ _____ $= 6$

$6 - 2 = $ _____

$6 - $ _____ $= 2$

2. $7 + 3 = $ _____

$3 + $ _____ $= 10$

$10 - $ _____ $= 3$

$10 - $ _____ $= 7$

3. $4 + 8 = $ _____

_____ $+ 4 = 12$

$12 - $ _____ $= 8$

_____ $- 8 = 4$

4. $3 + $ _____ $= 7$

_____ $+ $ _____ $= 7$

$7 - $ _____ $= 3$

_____ $- $ _____ $= 4$

5. $10 + 5 = $ _____

$5 + $ _____ $= $ _____

$15 - $ _____ $= $ _____

_____ $- 10 = $ _____

6. $6 + $ _____ $= 11$

_____ $+ $ _____ $= $ _____

_____ $- $ _____ $= 5$

_____ $- $ _____ $= $ _____

WORD WINDOW

Find the word in each pair that is spelled correctly and circle it.

becuase	said	befor
because	sead	before
they	once	wer
thay	wons	were
our	thare	pritty
uor	there	pretty

Complete each sentence. Use a word from the window above.

1. We _____ playing baseball outside.

2. Then _____ ball broke a window.

3. "Oh, no!" we all _____.

4. We must pay for the window _____ we broke it.

Day 45:
Sight Words and Spelling

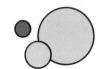

SIGN SEARCH

Figure out whether the equation needs a plus or a minus sign.
Write **+** or **−** in each equation.

1. $3 \boxed{} 4 = 7$

$8 \boxed{} 4 = 4$

2. $10 \boxed{} 1 = 11$

$10 \boxed{} 5 = 5$

3. $8 \boxed{} 3 = 5$

$9 \boxed{} 4 = 13$

4. $6 \boxed{} 7 = 13$

$16 \boxed{} 8 = 8$

5. $5 \boxed{} 9 = 14$

$9 \boxed{} 7 = 2$

6. $9 \boxed{} 8 = 17$

$5 \boxed{} 4 = 1$

7. $12 \boxed{} 7 = 5$

$8 \boxed{} 7 = 15$

8. $13 \boxed{} 3 = 10$

$3 \boxed{} 7 = 10$

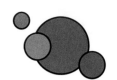

DRESSED TO DESCRIBE

An **adjective** describes something.

Sarah is wearing a **weird** outfit.

Circle the words that are adjectives.

hamburger	big	floppy	hold
short	wear	hat	hungry

Fill in the adjectives to describe what you see in the picture:

_____ pants   _____ shoes   _____ hat

Circle the adjective in each sentence.

1. Look at Sarah's wacky outfit.

2. Her pants have big dots.

3. She has a juicy burger.

4. It might drip on her fuzzy sweater.

Find each 3D shape in the picture below and circle it.

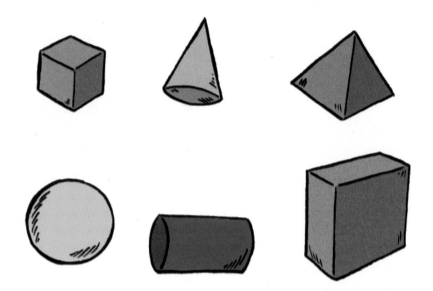

FOOD FOR THOUGHT

My favorite food is a peanut butter sandwich. The light brown bread feels soft. The peanut butter looks like thick frosting. It smells like fresh roasted peanuts and tastes creamy.

Now draw a picture of your favorite food.
Complete the sentences to write a descriptive paragraph.

My favorite food is _____.

It looks like _____.

When I touch it, it feels _____.

I can smell _____.

It tastes so _____.

 # DASHING DERBIES

Add or subtract. Find the answer on the derby track, and cross it out.
See which derby car wins the race!

A   **B**

 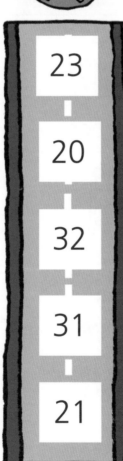

Track A: ~~33~~, 30, 11, 51, 22

Track B: 23, 20, 32, 31, 21

1.
$$
\begin{array}{r} 55 \\ -22 \\ \hline 33 \end{array}
$$

2.
$$
\begin{array}{r} 34 \\ -11 \\ \hline \end{array}
$$

3.
$$
\begin{array}{r} 76 \\ -46 \\ \hline \end{array}
$$

4.
$$
\begin{array}{r} 28 \\ -17 \\ \hline \end{array}
$$

5.
$$
\begin{array}{r} 40 \\ -20 \\ \hline \end{array}
$$

6.
$$
\begin{array}{r} 89 \\ -57 \\ \hline \end{array}
$$

7.
$$
\begin{array}{r} 93 \\ -42 \\ \hline \end{array}
$$

8.
$$
\begin{array}{r} 62 \\ -31 \\ \hline \end{array}
$$

9.
$$
\begin{array}{r} 39 \\ -17 \\ \hline \end{array}
$$

10.
$$
\begin{array}{r} 51 \\ -30 \\ \hline \end{array}
$$

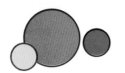
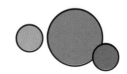

S STARTERS

Write the blend to complete each word. Use each blend twice.

sk	sl	sn	sm	sp	st

1.

___ ___op

2.

___ ___unk

3.

___ ___ake

4.

___ ___oon

5.

___ ___eep

6.

___ ___ar

7.

___ ___oke

8.

___ ___ide

9.

___ ___ill

10.

___ ___ail

11.

___ ___ell

12.

___ ___ate

List the words from above under the correct blend.

sk	sl	sn	sm	sp	st
_____	_____	_____	_____	_____	_____
_____	_____	_____	_____	_____	_____

Day 51:
S Blends

JUST JOKING

Add or subtract.

1. 44 − 33 S	**2.** 25 + 22 S	**3.** 63 − 43 E	**4.** 51 − 21 S
5. 51 + 36 T	**6.** 96 − 62 N	**7.** 38 − 17 N	**8.** 17 + 62 I
9. 58 + 31 H	**10.** 84 − 71 O	**11.** 77 + 21 E	

Find each number above and write the letter to answer the joke.

What kind of shoes do numbers wear?

T ___ ___ – ___ ___ ___
87 20 34   21 79 47

___ ___ ___ ___ ___
11 89 13 98 30

BOOK BASICS

Look at the Table of Contents. Then answer the questions.

Table of Contents

1. What is this book about? _____

2. How many chapters are in the book? _____

3. Which chapter is the shortest? _____

4. In which chapter would you read about craters on the moon's surface? _____

5. Which chapter explains how the moon affects the oceans on earth? _____

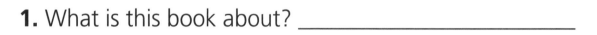

CAN YOU BUY IT?

Look at the price of each item and count the coins.
If you have enough money to buy it, circle **Yes**. If not, circle **No**.

1.     Yes (No)

2.    Yes No

3.     Yes No

4.    Yes No

5.    Yes No

6.    Yes No

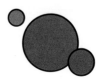

SHORT CUTS

Draw a line to connect each abbreviation with its matching word.

Dr.	Street
Jan.	Mister
St.	Doctor
Sun.	December
Dec.	Missus
Mr.	January
Ave.	Sunday
Mrs.	Avenue

Write each date using abbreviations.

1. Monday, February 6   _Mon., Feb. 6_

2. Tuesday, November 10   _____

3. Friday, October 2   _____

4. Saturday, August 8   _____

LET'S HALF FUN!

Does the picture have two equal halves?
If it does, draw a line dividing it into halves. If it doesn't, leave the picture blank.

1.

2.

3.

4.

Draw the other half of each picture.

5.

6.

SOCCER SENTENCES

Use capitals for:

- First word of a sentence
- Days of the week
- Months
- Titles like Mr. and Mrs.
- People's names

Every **S**aturday in **J**une, **M**rs. **J**ones coaches soccer.

Rewrite each sentence with correct capitalization. Don't forget to capitalize the first word in the sentence, the word "I" , and people's names.

1. on mondays i have soccer practice.

On Mondays I have soccer practice.

2. my coach is mrs. jones.

_____

3. every thursday we have a soccer game.

_____

4. our soccer team plays in april and may.

_____

5. in june there is a big game to end the season.

_____

6. even mr. jones comes to cheer on the team.

_____

TIC TAC TOE

Solve each story problem. Find the row that has three equal answers, and circle it.

1. Jill has five tulips, and Jon has six roses. How many flowers do they have altogether?

___11___ flowers

2. Ethan kicked five goals at the game, and so did Bruce. How many goals did they kick together?

_____ goals

3. Betty had twelve carrots. She gave six to Fran. How many carrots does Betty have left?

_____ carrots

4. Tom has two ladybugs, three beetles, and one cricket in his bug collection. How many bugs are there altogether?

_____ bugs

5. Brian had fifteen pieces of candy. He gave five to his brother. How many does he have left?

_____ pieces

6. The giant ice cream cone has two scoops of vanilla, two scoops of chocolate, and one scoop of strawberry. How many scoops does it have total?

_____ scoops

7. Lynn had sixteen stickers in her collection. She gave eight to Nora. How many stickers does Lynn have left?

_____ stickers

8. Drew scored seven points during the game. Then he scored three more during overtime. How many points total did he score?

_____ points

9. Dave has ten fingers and ten toes. How many fingers and toes does he have altogether?

_____ fingers and toes

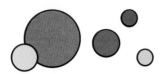

PEN PALS

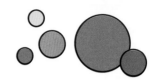

Think about something fun you've done this summer. Draw a picture of what you did.

Now write a letter to a friend or a family member by completing the sentences below.

Dear _____,

This summer, I went to _____.

While I was there, I saw _____ and _____.

I did some fun things, like _____. I also _____.

My favorite part was when we _____.

I will always remember this summer because _____.

Your friend,

_____

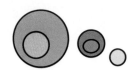

PLACE RACE

Count the groups of tens and ones, and write each number in standard form. Find each number in the racetrack, and cross it out. See which runner gets to the finish line first!

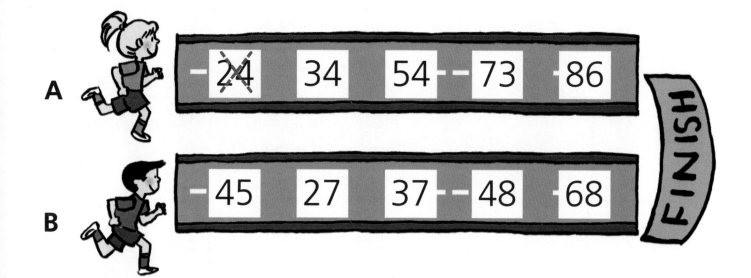

A ~~24~~ 34 54 73 86 FINISH

B 45 27 37 48 68

1.

2 tens + 4 ones = __24__

2.

3 tens + 4 ones = _____

3.

4 tens + 5 ones = _____

4.

5 tens + 4 ones = _____

5.

= _____

6.

= _____

7. 4 tens + 8 ones = _____

8. 7 tens + 3 ones = _____

9. 8 tens + 6 ones = _____

10. 6 tens + 8 ones = _____

BEGINNING BLENDS

Write the blend to complete each word. Use each blend once.

| bl | cl | fl | gl | pl | br | cr | dr | fr | gr | pr | tr |

1.

___ ___oom

2.

___ ___ue

3.

___ ___oud

4.

___ ___y

5.

___ ___og

6.

___ ___ass

7.

___ ___ock

8.

___ ___ince

9.

___ ___ag

10.

___ ___aw

11.

___ ___ane

12.

___ ___ain

Draw a line to connect the rhyming words.

plain   cry   blow   glass   press   free

fly   grow   tree   brain   class   dress

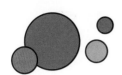

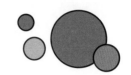

ADDITION ANTICS

Use regrouping to add.

```
  1
  12      Add the ones.
          8 + 2 = 10
+  8      Give 1 ten to the tens.
          Add the tens.
  20      1 + 1 = 2
```

1.
```
   1
   14
+  6
   20
```
D

2.
```
   16
+  5
```
R

3.
```
   28
+  4
```
E

4.
```
   19
+  4
```
I

5.
```
   25
+  5
```
D

6.
```
   37
+  7
```
A

7.
```
   36
+  6
```
I

8.
```
   46
+  4
```
M

Find each number above and write the letter to complete the joke.

What did the number write on the valentine card?

```
 I   ___  ___  ___  ___  ___  ___
23    44   30   20   50   42   21   32
```

YOU!

OUR NATIONAL ANTHEM

Read the story. Then look at each sentence below and circle **True** or **False**.

Francis Scott Key lived during the time of the Revolutionary War. One night, he was on a ship in the Baltimore Harbor. The British came to Fort McHenry that night. Francis watched the battle all night. In the morning, there was lots of smoke, but Francis could still see the American flag flying. He wrote a poem about the flag. This poem later became the song the "Star Spangled Banner." Francis Scott Key helped to give America this important song!

1. Francis Scott Key's poem became the song "The Star Spangled Banner."   True   False

2. Francis fought at Fort McHenry when the British came.   True   False

3. Francis watched the soldiers fighting all night long.   True   False

4. In the morning, Francis could see only smoke.   True   False

5. The song "The Star Spangled Banner" is about the flag.   True   False

WHAT'S YOUR FAVORITE MEAL?

Ask ten people what their favorite meal of the day is.
Color in the rectangles to show how many people chose each meal.
Start coloring at the bottom. Then answer the questions below.

	breakfast	lunch	dinner
10			
9			
8			
7			
6			
5			
4			
3			
2			
1			

1. What is this graph about? _____

2. Which meal did the most people like? _____

3. Which meal did the fewest people like? _____

4. How many people said lunch was their favorite meal? _____

PUZZLING PLURALS

Write the plural for each word.

To show more than one, drop the letter **y** and add the letters **ies**.

 cher**y** ~~x~~   cher**ies**

1.

pony _____

2.

baby _____

3.

berry _____

4.

daddy _____

Circle the correct plural for each word.

5. man   **a)** mans   **b)** men   **c)** mens

6. foot   **a)** footes   **b)** foots   **c)** feet

7. mouse   **a)** mice   **b)** mouses   **c)** mousies

8. tooth   **a)** tooths   **b)** teeth   **c)** toothes

Day 65:
Irregular Plurals

TELL THE TIME

Write the time below each clock.

 [15 min]

To show 15 minutes past the hour, the big hand points to the 3.

 [15 min]

[45 min]

[30 min]

To show 45 minutes past the hour, the big hand points to the 9. The little hand is almost pointing to the next number.

1.

2:15

2.

_____

3.

_____

4.

_____

5.

_____

6.

_____

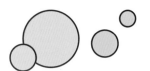
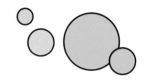

Posessives show something belongs to someone.

The cap belongs to Pam.
Pam**'s** cap

Pronouns stand in place of names.

He   She   They   It

Sam is a boy. **He** likes music.

Write who it belongs to. Then write the possessive.

1. The flute belongs to ____Sam____.   ____Sam's____ flute

2. The bat belongs to _____.   _____ bat

3. The baseball belongs to _____.   _____ baseball

4. The music belongs to _____.   _____ music

Circle the person's name. Then circle the pronoun. Write who the pronoun stands for.

5. Sam plays the flute.
He likes music.
____Sam____

6. Pam plays baseball.
She likes sports.
_____

7. Sam and Pam are friends.
They like to play.
_____

8. Sam is dressed up.
He is wearing a tie.
_____

RING TOSS

Figure out the number pattern in each row. Continue the pattern and fill in the empty rings with the last two numbers. Use the rings at the bottom for help.

2	4	6	8	10	12
5	10	15	20		
1	3	5	7		
3	6	9	12		
4	8	12	16		

30   10   12   20   11

9   18   24   15   25

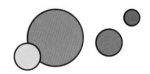
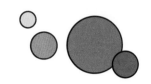

PRACTICE TIME

Practice writing the letters in cursive.

Aa   Aa - - - - - - - - - - - - - - - -

Bb   Bb - - - - - - - - - - - - - - - -

Cc   Cc - - - - - - - - - - - - - - - -

Dd   Dd - - - - - - - - - - - - - - - -

Ee   Ee - - - - - - - - - - - - - - - -

Ff   Ff - - - - - - - - - - - - - - - -

Gg   Gg - - - - - - - - - - - - - - - -

Hh   Hh - - - - - - - - - - - - - - - -

Ii   Ii - - - - - - - - - - - - - - - -

Now practice writing your name in cursive

- -

- -

**Day 69:
Handwriting A–I**

 # RAFT RACE

Find the word to complete each sentence. Cross out each word as you use it.
The raft with all its words crossed out first wins the race.

1. My backpack weighs ten
   _____pounds_____.

2. The pencil is six _____
   long.

3. The pool is eight _____
   deep.

4. The popcorn popped in three
   _____.

5. There are seven _____
   in one week.

6. The lollipop costs ten _____.

7. A football field is 100 _____
   long.

8. A nickel weighs about $\frac{1}{5}$ of an
   _____.

9. The plane ride to New York
   took six _____.

10. My new T-shirt costs ten
    _____.

feet
minutes
yards
pounds
dollars

days
inches
ounce
cents
hours

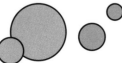

PHONICS FUN

Write the blend to complete each word. Use each blend three times.

ch	sh	th	wh

1. ___ ___ip

2. ___ ___eel

3. ___ ___umb

4. ___ ___ree

5. ___ ___istle

6. ___ ___oe

7. ___ ___air

8. ___ ___in

9. ___ ___eese

10. ___ ___eek

11. ___ ___ell

12. ___ ___ale

List the words from above under the correct blend.

ch	sh	th	wh
_____	_____	_____	_____
_____	_____	_____	_____
_____	_____	_____	_____

Day 71:
Digraphs ch, sh, th, wh

LAUGH IT OFF

Use regrouping to subtract.

$^1_1$
$\cancel{2}2$
$-\ 6$
$\overline{\ \ 6}$ Take 1 from the tens.
$12 - 6 = 6$ → ^{1}
$\cancel{2}2$ Now subtract the tens.
$1 - 0 = 1$

1.
$^1_1$
$\cancel{2}6$
$-\ 9$
$\overline{17}$

I

2.
23
$-\ 5$

A

3.
31
$-\ 8$

H

4.
35
$-\ 6$

N

5.
44
$-\ 7$

B

6.
22
$-\ 6$

G

7.
46
$-\ 8$

S

8.
31
$-\ 5$

D

Find each number above and write the letter to complete the joke.

If you have seven apples in one hand and five in the other, what do you have?

$\underline{B}$ $\underline{\ \ \ \ }$ $\underline{\ \ \ \ }$ $\underline{\ \ \ \ }$ $\underline{\ \ \ \ }$ $\underline{\ \ \ \ }$ $\underline{\ \ \ \ }$ $\underline{\ \ \ \ }$!
37   17   16   23   18   29   26   38

A DOG'S DAY

Read the story. Then answer the questions.

Dogs are fun to play catch with or to curl up with on the couch. Yet having a pet dog isn't all fun and games. It's a lot of hard work, too.

A pet dog relies on its owner for food, water, and exercise every day. Someone has to fill the food bowl and take the dog for walks. Dogs also need checkups at the vet and shots to stay healthy.

A pet dog can be a special friend if you are ready for the responsibilities.

1. What is the main idea of the passage?
  a) Playing catch with a dog can be a lot of fun.
  b) Owning a dog comes with many responsibilities.

2. What is the author's purpose?
  a) To prove that having a pet dog is hard work.
  b) To inform the reader about what dogs eat.

3. List some of the things a dog owner must do.

_____

_____

_____

_____

4. Would you like to have a pet dog? Why or why not?

_____

_____

_____

_____

Day 73:
Main Idea

 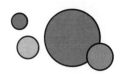

IT'S ABOUT TIME

Figure out how much time passed, and write it on the line.

1. 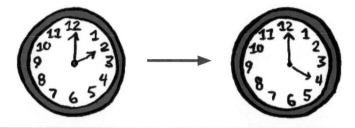 = __2 hours__

2. 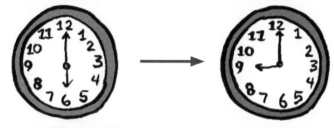 = _____

3. 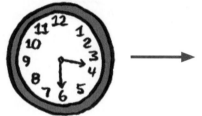 = _____

Draw the hands to show the start and the finish times.

4.

START

Jon started his test at 10:00.
He finished 30 minutes later.

FINISH

5.

START

The game started at 2:15.
It finished 2 hours later.

FINISH

6.

START

Meg's party started at 11:30.
It finished 3 hours later.

FINISH

SAY IT AGAIN

Synonyms are words that mean almost the same thing.
Connect each word with its synonym.

1. little   speedy   **4.** laugh   mad

2. run   jog   **5.** angry   glad

3. fast   small   **6.** happy   giggle

Look at the underlined word in each sentence. Find the word in the box
that means almost the same thing. Write it on the line.

chatted	tasty	cooked	cold	feast

7. My whole family got together for a <u>barbecue</u>. _____feast_____

8. We <u>roasted</u> hot dogs over a fire. _____

9. The corn on the cob was so <u>yummy</u>! _____

10. The root beer was <u>chilled</u>. _____

11. I <u>talked</u> with my cousins. _____

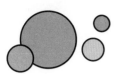 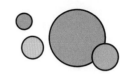

FRACTION FUN

Color one half of the items in each box.

1.

2.

3.

4.

Shade one piece of pie in each picture to equal the fraction.

5. $\frac{1}{2}$

6. $\frac{1}{3}$

7. $\frac{1}{4}$

8. $\frac{1}{2}$

Unscramble the words and write the sentence.

1. camped lake . the I at

_____

2. up tent . We put a

_____

3. bag . I in slept sleeping a

_____

4. . over fire We a cooked

_____

5. fishing I went the . lake in

_____

6. so fun much . We had

_____

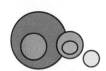 

GOODY BAGS

Divide up the treats equally. How many can you put in each bag? Use tally marks to keep track. Write the number per bag on the line to solve the problem.

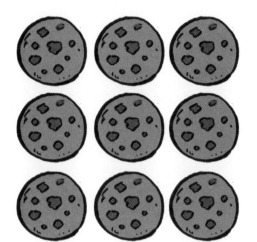

$9 \div 3 = \underline{3}$

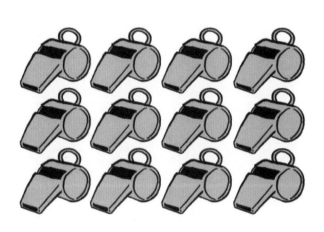

$12 \div 2 = \underline{}$

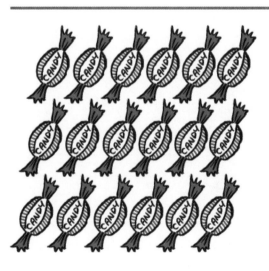

$15 \div 3 = \underline{}$

TIME TO WRITE

Practice writing the letters in cursive.

Jj — *Jj* — — — — — — —

Kk — *Kk* — — — — — — —

Ll — *Ll* — — — — — — —

Mm — *Mm* — — — — — —

Nn — *Nn* — — — — — —

Oo — *Oo* — — — — — — —

Pp — *Pp* — — — — — — —

Qq — *Qq* — — — — — — —

Rr — *Rr* — — — — — — —

Copy the number words in cursive.

one — — — — — — — *two* — — — — — —

three — — — — — *four* — — — — —

TRICKY TRACKS

Which track should the runner use? Use regrouping to add or subtract.
Then find the racetrack that has all the correct answers to the problems.

A **B**

A	B
44	16
21	28
31	31
18	12
16	40
28	24
17	23
32	21

1. 14
     + 7

2. 22
     − 4

3. 23
     + 9

4. 25
     − 9

5. 38
     + 6

6. 33
     − 5

7. 25
     + 6

8. 24
     − 7

FAMILY TREE

Complete the word family lists using words from inside the tree.
Then come up with one of your own words for each list.

went   punch
call   told   light
lunch
cold
wall
sent
night

ball
_____
_____
_____

munch
_____
_____
_____

gold
_____
_____
_____

tight
_____
_____
_____

tent
_____
_____
_____

truck   land
long   wrong
luck
kick
best
hand
test
pick

band
_____
_____
_____

west
_____
_____
_____

lick
_____
_____
_____

song
_____
_____
_____

duck
_____
_____
_____

Day 81:
Word Families

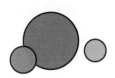
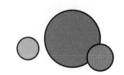

GROUPS OF GRAPES

Count the number of groups and the number of grapes.
Solve the multiplication problems.

- 4 grapes in the group
- 1 group

4 x 1 = 4

1.

- 3 grapes
- 1 group

3 x 1 = _____

B

2.

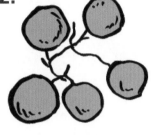

- 5 grapes
- 1 group

5 x 1 = _____

T

3.

- 2 grapes
- 1 group

2 x 1 = _____

S

4.

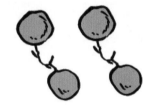

- 2 grapes
- 2 groups

2 x 2 = _____

A

5.

- 4 grapes
- 2 groups

4 x 2 = _____

L

6.

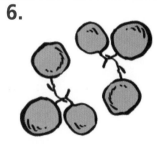

- 3 grapes
- 2 groups

3 x 2 = _____

E

Find each number above, and write the letter to complete the joke.

Where do the students sit during math class?

At the times ____ ____ B ____ ____ ____
           5   4   3   8   6   2

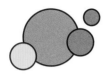
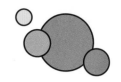

THE CAR WASH

Read the story. Then answer the questions.

Emily's team wanted to go to soccer camp in the summer. The team members decided to have a car wash to raise money. They needed a way to spread the word. Emily helped to put posters and flyers all around town. Everyone hoped the car wash would be a success.

On the day of the car wash, cars were lined up around the block! The girls split into two groups so they could wash the cars twice as fast. By the end of the day, the girls had raised enough money. The team would be able to go to soccer camp!

Connect each cause with its effect.

Cause

1. The team needed money for soccer camp.

2. They wanted to spread the word about the car wash.

3. Cars were lined up around the block.

4. The girls washed enough cars to raise the money.

Effect

a) The team would be able to go to soccer camp.

b) The team members decided to have a car wash.

c) The girls split into two groups to work faster.

d) Emily helped to put posters and flyers around town.

**Day 83:
Cause and Effect**

PAW PAIRS

Find each paw print in the graph. First, count how many rows to the right.
Then, count how many rows up. Write the number pair that shows the location.

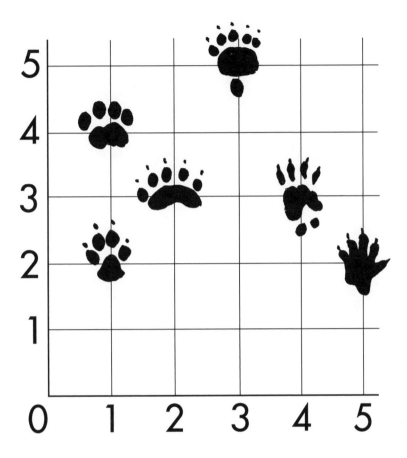

1. _1_, _2_

2. _____, _____

3. _____, _____

4. _____, _____

5. _____, _____

6. _____, _____

BEACH DAY

Antonyms are words that mean the opposite. Connect each word with its antonym.

1. short   go

2. stop   tall

3. light   dark

4. sad   out

5. high   low

6. in   happy

Find two words in each sentence that are antonyms. Underline the words.

7. We jumped over the waves and swam under the water.

8. The cold water felt good on a hot day.

9. Our swimsuits were wet, but our towels were dry.

10. We found tiny shells and put them in a big bucket.

11. We went home when the day was turning into night.

12. As the sun slowly set, we quickly left the beach.

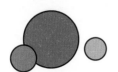 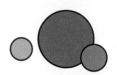

SHIFTING SHAPES

Shapes can be put together to make new shapes.

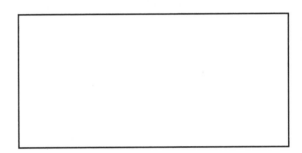

Draw a line to divide each shape into the shapes listed below.

1.

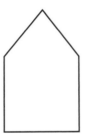

2 triangles

2.

2 squares

3.

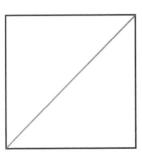

A square and a triangle

4.

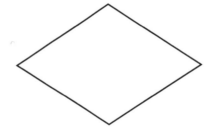

2 triangles

5.

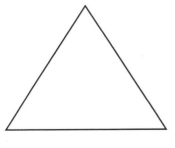

2 triangles

6.

2 rectangles

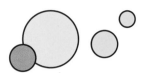
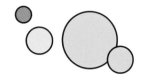

SPEAK UP!

Quotation marks show the exact words that a speaker says. They go at the beginning and the end of the speaker's words, after the punctuation mark.

Connor said, "I love this movie."
"Me, too," Tony said.

Underline the words that the speaker says. Then put quote marks around them.

1. Conner whispered to Tony, "Be quiet please."

2. Tony replied, What did you say?

3. Conner asked, Can you eat your popcorn quietly?

4. Tony answered, I still can't hear you.

5. Your popcorn is too loud! Conner shouted.

6. Tony replied, Well, why didn't you speak up?

 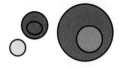

THREE IN A ROW

Look at each picture and figure out whether it shows $\frac{1}{2}$, $\frac{1}{3}$, or $\frac{1}{4}$. Write the fraction in each box. Find three in a row with the same answer and circle the row.

1.

2.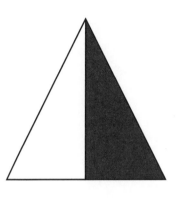

3.

4.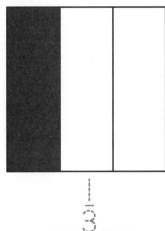

5.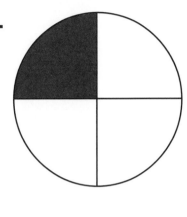

6.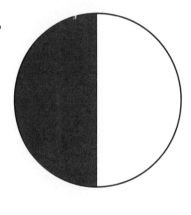

7.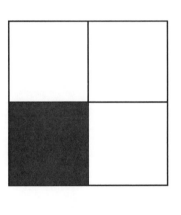

8.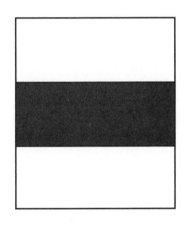

9.

WRITE AWAY

Practice writing the letters in cursive.

Ss   Ss

Tt   Tt

Uu   Uu

Vv   Vv

Ww   Ww

Xx   Xx

Yy   Yy

Zz   Zz

Copy the days of the week in cursive.

Monday _____   Tuesday _____

Wednesday _____   Thursday _____

Friday _____   Saturday _____

Sunday _____

RUN FOR THE MONEY

Rounding numbers is easy! Here's how you do it.

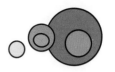

When you use the $ sign, money less than one dollar goes after the decimal point.

1¢ = $.01   5¢ = $.05   10¢ = $.10

Help the runner win the race. Find the correct statements
to make a path through the maze.

35¢ = $3.50

10¢ = $1.00

25¢ = $.25

60¢ = $.06

4¢ = $.40

7¢ = $7.00

15¢ = $.15   3¢ = $.03   20¢ = $.20

50¢ = $.50

8¢ = $.08

ANSWER KEY

Page 4
2. q r s
3. i j k
4. u v w
5. c d e
6. g h i
7. m n o
8. s t u
9. k l m
10. o p q
11. x y z
12. a b c
13. A B C ~~D~~ D E F G
14. L M N O ~~P~~ P Q R
15. T U V W ~~X~~ X Y Z

Page 5
3 4 5   8 9 10   18 19 20
11 12 13   6 7 8   14 15 16

12 13 14 15 16
21 22 23 24 25

8 7 6 5 4
20 19 18 17 16

Where do numbers like to each lunch?
AT THE COUNTER

Page 6
1. a
2. a
3. b
4. b

Page 7
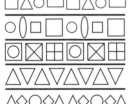

Page 8
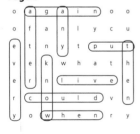

Page 9
1. 4 5   2. 2 4
   +3 +1   +6 +0
   (7) 6   (8) 4

3. 1 3   4. 0 2
   +7 +3   +5 +2
   (8) 6   (5) 4

5. 4 2   6. 1 8
   +1 +8   +6 +1
   5 (10)   7 (9)

7. 5 5   8. 0 3
   +4 +5   +9 +7
   9 (10)   9 (10)

Page 10
2. I left my lunch at home.
3. I can share my lunch.
4. Do you like apples?
5. Can I have a bite?
6. You are a good friend.

Page 11

Bottom:
5 10 15 20 25 30 35 40 45 50
55 60 65 70 75 80 85 90 95 100

Page 12
1. This is my pet bird.
2.–3. Answers will vary.
4. What does the bird eat?
5.–6. Answers will vary.

Page 13
1. 8   2. 5
   −4   −2
    4   3

3. 4   4. 9
   −2   −3
    2   6

5. 9   6. 10
   −1   −5
    8   5

7. 6   8. 9
   −5   −2
    1   7

9. 9   10. 12
   −0   −2
    9   10

Winner: Rocket A

Page 14
2. cup
3. hat
4. jam
5. web
6. lid
7. zip
8. rug
9. van
10. Beginning
11. Ending
12. Beginning

Page 15
51 52 53 54 55 56 57 58 59 60
61 62 63 64 65 66 67 68 69 70
71 72 73 74 75 76 77 78 79 80
81 82 83 84 85 86 87 88 89 90
91 92 93 94 95 96 97 98 99 100

How high did the silly clown count?
TO ONE FUNDRED

Page 16
The course started with some easy holes. 3
Andy and his friends went to the mini golf course. 1
The hole was on a narrow bridge above the water. 5
They rented clubs and balls and started the game. 2
Andy's ball rolled off the bridge and splashed into the water. 6
Then they got to a very tricky hole surrounded by water. 4
1. c
2. a
3. d
4. b

Page 17

5¢
10¢
25¢
10¢
15¢

Page 18
1. I found my lucky racing socks.
2. It was time for the bike race!
3. I raced along a path lined with trees.
4. I saw two foxes playing in the woods.
5. There were sharp rocks on the ground.
6. I thought that I had a flat tire.
7. It was just a rock stuck in my wheel.
8. I finished the race and got a ribbon.

Page 19
1. 2 + 3 = 5   2. 6 + 4 = 10
   3 + 2 = 5   4 + 6 = 10
3. 5 + 2 = 7   4. 2 + 9 = 11
   2 + 5 = 7   9 + 2 = 11
5. 6 + 3 = 9   6. 9 + 1 = 10
   3 + 6 = 9   1 + 9 = 10
7. 7 + 5 = 12   8. 3 + 8 = 11
   5 + 7 = 12   8 + 3 = 11

Page 20
2. Our plane landed in Honolulu.
3. Then Amy and I flew to Maui.
4. Amy's sister Peg lives in Maui.
5. Peg took Amy and me swimming.
6. I want to go to Hawaii again!

Page 21
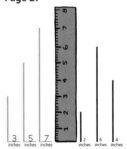

Answers will vary.

Page 22
Answers will vary.

Page 23
Cobras are the winner.
1. 10:00   2. 2:30   3. 4:30
4. 6:00   5. 8:00   6. 5:30
7. 7:00   8. 11:00 9. 12:30

Page 24
2. tube
3. cane
4. tape
5. hid
6. hope
7. fine
8. bit
9. not
10. mope
11. mad
12. rode

Page 25
1. 2   2. 5   3. 2
    4   2   3
   +1   +2   +3
    7   9   8

4. 4   5. 8   6. 6
    2   3   3
   +4   +3   +2
   10   14   11

7. 9   8. 3   9. 7
    3   4   5
   +1   +5   +3
   13   12   15

What did the 0 say to the 8?
NICE BELT!

Page 26
2. Was very artistic (Larry)
3. Earned money to buy flowers (Gary)
4. Worked hard to give a nice present (Both)
5. Painted a picture of a flower garden (Larry)
6. Had good business ideas (Gary)

Page 27

8
7
6
5
4
3
2
1
3   5   7   2   6   4
inches inches inches   inches inches inches

Page 28
rain —— room
bed —— fly
snow —— ball
butter —— bow
side —— man
foot —— walk

1. butterfly
2. football
3. bedroom
4. snowman
5. sidewalk
6. rainbow

Page 29
1. 5 apples
2. 4 cookies
3. 11 toppings
4. 10 fries
5. 12 berries
6. 8 chips

Page 30
Top:
write (boy) (cap) sit
smart (pencil) (paper) read

Middle:
Answers may vary.
pen, ruler, book, schoolwork, crayons, paperclips, desk

Bottom:
2. Open your (book) please.
3. Take out a (pen)
4. Use some (paper) for writing.

Page 31

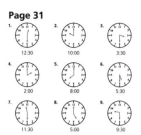

1. 12:30 2. 10:00 3. 3:30
4. 2:00 5. 8:00 6. 5:30
7. 11:30 8. 5:00 9. 9:30

Message: CHOCO-LATE

Page 32
Answers will vary.

Page 33

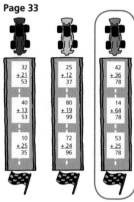

32
+ 21
53

25
+ 12
37

42
+ 36
78

40
+ 13
53

80
+ 19
99

14
+ 64
78

10
+ 25
35

72
+ 24
96

53
+ 25
78

Page 34
2. bee
3. rain
4. pie
5. bike
6. toe
7. tube
8. cry
9. glue
10. boat
11. hay
12. bow
13. cake
14. leaf

long a: rain, hay, cake
long e: bee, leaf
long i: pie, bike, cry
long o: rose, toe, boat, bow
long u: tube, glue

Page 35
2 4 6 8 10
12 14 16 18 20
22 24 26 28 30

10 20 30 40 50
60 70 80 90 100

Where did the numbers have a picnic?
IN THE FOUR-EST

Page 36
1. b
2. Snakes, mosquitoes, alligators.
3. Answers may vary.
   It is hot, steamy, and damp.
4. Answers will vary.

Page 37

Page 38
Top:
can't — is not
won't — could not
isn't — will not
aren't — are not
couldn't — did not
didn't — can not

Bottom:
2. I could not hear the alarm. couldn't
3. I can not be late to school. can't
4. My parents are not going to like this. aren't
5. The bus is not going to wait. isn't
6. I will not get to school on time! won't

Page 39
1. 3 < 30   2. 10 > 3+1
   21 = 21   6 < 5+4
   44 > 14   8 = 3+5
3. 2+1 < 2+2   4. 7+1 < 4+5
   3+4 > 6+0   5+1 = 3+3
   2+8 = 8+2   4+2 > 3+1
5. 5–3 < 6–2   6. 8–7 = 5–4
   8–3 > 7–5   4–0 > 7–4
   6–3 > 10–7   8–8 < 7–2
7. 1+4 = 10–5 8. 10–4 < 4+4
   6+2 > 6–3   9–5 = 2+2
   2+0 < 10–7   6–1 > 3+0

Page 40
cake (sing) birthday (clap)
party candles (melt) (blow)

Middle:
Action words will vary.

Bottom:
1. Molly (closes) her eyes.
2. Her friends (shout) "Happy Birthday!"
3. Everyone (eats) a lot of cake.
4. Then Molly (opens) her gifts.

Page 41

Crossword:
t w o
six
one
seven
eight
three
ten
nine
five
four

Why did the boy lose his money?
Because he had no CENTS.

Across
1. 5 + 1 = 6
2. 8 – 7 = 1
3. 10 – 2 = 8
4. 3 + 7 = 10
5. 11 – 6 = 5

Down
1. 9 – 7 = 2
2. 2 + 5 = 7
3. 9 – 6 = 3
4. 3 + 6 = 9
5. 12 – 8 = 4

Page 42
Answers will vary.

Page 43

19 32 42 81 16
22 52 11 70 61

1. 17   2. 24   3. 58
   – 4   – 2   – 6
   13   22   52

4. 35   5. 47   6. 88
   – 3   – 5   – 7
   32   42   81

7. 19   8. 73   9. 66
   – 8   – 3   – 5
   11   70   61

Page 44
Answers may vary.
2. pen, hen, ten; short e
3. sit, bit, kit; short i
4. mop, cop, top; short o
5. mug, hug, rug; short u
6. bake, cake, lake; long a
7. heat, neat, beat; long e
8. dine, nine, vine; long i
9. rope, hope, cope; long o
10. true, blue, glue; long u
11. snack
12. moon
13. head
14. broom

Page 45

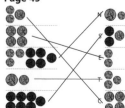

Page 46
1. 200 million
2. b) 2/3 cup dish detergent and c) 1 gallon water
3. can, hanger, hula hoop
4. 2–Mix in 2/3 cup of dish detergent.
   1–Pour a gallon of water into a large tray.
   4–Wave it in the air.
   3–Dip a can, a hanger, or a hula hoop into the mixture.

Page 47
1. 4 + 2 = 6   2. 7 + 3 = 10
   2 + 4 = 6   3 + 7 = 10
   6 – 2 = 4   10 – 7 = 3
   6 – 4 = 2   10 – 3 = 7

3. 4 + 8 = 12   4. 3 + 4 = 7
   8 + 4 = 12   4 + 3 = 7
   12 – 4 = 8   7 – 4 = 3
   12 – 8 = 4   7 – 3 = 4

5. 10 + 5 = 15 6. 6 + 5 = 11
   5 + 10 = 15   5 + 6 = 11
   15 – 5 = 10   11 – 6 = 5
   15 – 10 = 5   11 – 5 = 6

Page 48
becuase (said) befor
(because) sead (before)

(they) (once) wer
thay wons (were)

(our) thare pritty
uor (there) (pretty)

1. We were playing baseball outside.
2. Then our ball broke a window.
3. "Oh, no!" we all said.
4. We must pay for the window because we broke it.

Page 49
1. 3 + 4 = 7   2. 10 + 1 = 11
   8 – 4 = 4   5 – 5 = 5
3. 8 – 3 = 5   4. 6 + 7 = 13
   9 + 4 = 13   16 – 8 = 8
5. 5 + 9 = 14   6. 9 + 8 = 17
   9 – 7 = 2   5 – 4 = 1
7. 12 – 7 = 5   8. 13 – 3 = 10
   8 + 7 = 15   3 + 7 = 10

Page 50
hamburger (big) (floppy) hold
(short) wear hat (hungry)

Answers will vary.
long pants, high shoes, pretty hat

2. Her pants have (big) dots.
3. She has a (juicy) burger.
4. It might drip on her (fuzzy) sweater.

Page 51

Page 52
Answers will vary.

Page 53
1. 55   2. 34
   – 22   – 11
   33   23

3. 76   4. 28
   – 46   – 17
   30   11

5. 40   6. 89
   – 20   – 57
   20   32

7. 93   8. 62
   – 42   – 31
   51   31

9. 39   10. 51
   – 17   – 30
   22   21

Race car A wins.

Page 54
1. stop 2. skunk 3. snake
4. spoon 5. sleep 6. star
7. smoke 8. slide 9. spill
10. snail 11. smell 12. skate

sk: skunk, skate
sl: sleep, slide
sn: snake, snail
sm: smoke, smell
sp: spoon, spill
st: stop, star

Page 55
1. 25   2. 25   3. 63   4. 51
   – 33   + 22   – 43   – 21
   11   47   20   30

5. 51   6. 96   7. 38   8. 17
   + 36   – 62   – 17   + 62
   87   34   21   79

9. 58   10. 84   11. 77
   + 31   – 71   + 21
   89   13   98

What kind of shoes do numbers wear?
TEN -NIS SHOES

Page 56
1. The moon
2. Five
3. Chapter 3
4. Chapter 1
5. Chapter 4

Page 57
2. Yes
3. No
4. Yes
5. Yes
6. No

Page 58

Dr. — Street
Jan. — Mister
St. — Doctor
Sun. — December
Dec. — Misuss
Mr. — January
Ave. — Sunday
Mrs. — Avenue

2. Tues., Nov. 10
3. Fri., Oct. 2
4. Sat., Aug. 8

Page 59

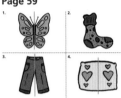

Page 60

2. My coach is Mrs. Jones.
3. Every Thursday we have a soccer game.
4. Our soccer team plays in April and May.
5. In June there is a big game to end the season.
6. Even Mr. Jones comes to cheer on the team.

Page 61

11	10	6
6	10	5
8	10	20

Page 62

Answers will vary.

Page 63

2. 34
3. 45
4. 54
5. 27
6. 37
7. 48
8. 73
9. 86
10. 68

Runner A wins.

Page 64

1. broom   2. glue   3. cloud
4. cry   5. frog   6. grass
7. block   8. prince 9. flag
10. draw   11. plane 12. train

Page 65

1. 14   2. 16   3. 28   4. 19
   +6   +5   +4   +4
   20   21   32   23

5. 25   6. 37   7. 36   8. 46
   +5   +7   +6   +4
   30   44   42   50

What did the number write on the valentine card?
I ADDMIRE YOU!

Page 66

1. True
2. False
3. True
4. False
5. True

Page 67

1. Favorite meals
2.–4. Answers will vary.

Page 68

1. ponies   2. babies
3. berries   4. daddies
5. b
6. c
7. a
8. b

Page 69

1. 2:15   2. 3:15
3. 5:45   4. 10:45
5. 7:15   6. 11:45

Page 70

2. The bat belongs to Pam. Pam's bat
3. The baseball belongs to Pam. Pam's baseball
4. The music belongs to Sam. Sam's music

6. Pam plays baseball. She likes sports. Pam
7. Sam and Pam are friends. They like to play. Sam and Pam
8. Sam is dressed up. He is wearing a tie. Sam

Page 71

5   10   15   20   25   30
1   3   5   7   9   11
3   6   9   12   15   18
4   8   12   16   20   24

Page 73

2. inches
3. feet
4. minutes
5. days
6. cents
7. yards
8. ounce
9. hours
10. dollars

Page 74

1. ship   2. wheel   3. thumb
4. three   5. whistle 6. shoe
7. chair   8. thin   9. cheese
10. cheek 11. shell   12. whale

ch: chair, cheese, cheek
sh: ship, shoe, shell
th: thumb, three, thin
wh: wheel, whistle, whale

Page 75

1. 26   2. 23   3. 31   4. 35
   -9   -5   -8   -6
   17   18   23   29

5. 44   6. 22   7. 46   8. 31
   -7   -6   -8   -5
   37   16   38   26

If you have seven apples in one hand and five in the other, what do you have?
BIG HANDS!

Page 76

1. b
2. a
3. An owner needs to give a dog food, water, exercise, and take it to the vet for checkups and shots.
4. Answers will vary.

Page 77

2. 3 hours
3. 1 hour
4.

5.

6.

Page 78

1. little — speedy
2. run — jog
3. fast — small
4. laugh — mad
5. angry — glad
6. happy — giggle

8. cooked
9. tasty
10. cold
11. chatted

Page 79

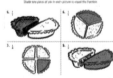
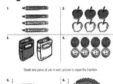

Page 80

1. I camped at the lake.
2. We put up a tent.
3. I slept in a sleeping bag.
4. We cooked over a fire.
5. I went fishing in the lake.
6. We had so much fun.

Page 81

12 ÷ 2 = 6

15 ÷ 3 = 5

Page 83

1.   14   2.   22
     + 7   - 4
      21   18

3.   23   4.   25
     + 9   - 9
      32   16

5.   38   6.   33
     + 6   - 6
      44   28

7.   25   8.   24
     + 6   - 7
      31   17

Runner should use track A.

Page 84

Top:
ball   munch
wall   lunch
call   punch
Answers vary.   Answers vary.

gold   tight
cold   night
told   light
Answers vary.   Answers vary.

tent
went
sent
Answers vary.

Bottom:
band   west
hand   best
land   test
Answers vary.   Answers vary.

lick   song
kick   long
pick   wrong
Answers vary.   Answers vary.

duck
truck
luck
Answers vary.

Page 85

2. 5 X 1 = 5
3. 2 X 1 = 2
4. 2 X 2 = 4
5. 4 X 2 = 8
6. 3 X 2 = 6

Where did the students sit during math class?
At the times TABLES

Page 86

2. d
3. c
4. a

Page 87

1. 1,2   2. 4,3
3. 2,3   4. 5,2
5. 3,5   6. 1,4

Page 88

1. short — go
2. stop — tall
3. light — dark
4. sad — out
5. high — low
6. in — happy
7. We jumped over the waves and swam under the water.
8. The cold water felt good on a hot day.
9. Our swimsuits were wet but our towels were dry.
10. We found tiny shells and put them in a big bucket.
11. We went home when the day was turning into night.
12. As the sun slowly set, we quickly left the beach.

Page 89

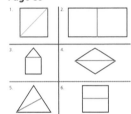

Page 90

2. Tony replied, "What did you say?"
3. Conner asked, "Can you eat your popcorn quietly?"
4. Tony answered, "I still can't hear you."
5. "Your popcorn is too loud!" shouted Conner.
6. Tony replied, "Well, why didn't you speak up?"

Page 91

1. 1/3	2. 1/4	3. 1/2
4. 1/4	5. 1/3	6. 1/2
7. 1/2	8. 1/4	9. 1/3

Page 93

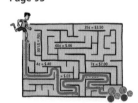